# AUTOMATIC PILOT

**ERIKA RITTER**

**Playwrights Canada Press**
**Toronto**

*PLAYWRIGHTS CANADA PRESS* is the imprint of PLAYWRIGHTS UNION OF CANADA.
PLAYWRIGHTS UNION OF CANADA
54 Wolseley Street, 2nd floor
Toronto, Ontario
Canada, M5T 1A5
Phone (416) 947-0201
Fax (416) 947-0159



PLAYWRIGHTS CANADA PRESS operates with generous assistance from the Canada Council, the Department of External Affairs, the Ontario Ministry of Culture and Communications, the Ontario Arts Council, the Municipality of Metropolitan Toronto—Cultural Affairs Division, and the City of Toronto through the Toronto Arts Council.

*Front cover photo by Andrew Oxenham.*
*Designed and edited by Tony Hamill.*
*Typeset by Thompson Educational Publishing, Inc.*

Canadian Cataloguing in Publication Data
Ritter, Erika, 1948-
Automatic pilot
A play.
3rd Edition
ISBN 0-88754-473-8
I. Title.
PS8585.I8A87 1991 C812'.54 C91-095378-3
PR9199.3.R57A87 1991

First edition: April 1980
Second edition: May 1984
Third edition: December 1991
Printed and bound by Canadian Printco Ltd.

# AUTOMATIC PILOT

*Automatic Pilot* was first produced by The New Theatre at The Court Theatre, Adelaide Court, Toronto, in January 1980, with the following cast:

| | |
|---|---|
| CHARLIE | *Fiona Reid* |
| GENE | *Geoffrey Bowes* |
| NICK | *John Evans* |
| ALAN | *Patrick Young* |

*Directed by William Lane.*
*Set Design by Roderick Hillier.*

*Automatic Pilot* transferred to the Toronto Free Theatre in February 1980 with one cast change:

| | |
|---|---|
| ALAN | *David McIlwraith* |

The Characters

CHARLIE, *30*
GENE, *23*
NICK, *35*
ALAN, *30*

The Time: 1980

The Setting

*Toronto, Canada. The action takes place over approximately two months in the late summer and early fall.*

N.B. References to prices and other expenses are in the value of the dollar in 1980.

## Act One, Scene One

*Lights come up on the area of the stage designated as The Canada Goose, a comedy club, suggested by a mike on a stand and a spotlight.* CHARLIE, *dressed simply in a blouse and jeans, and without her glasses, stands nervously at the mike, speaking awkwardly into it without daring to remove it from the stand.*

**CHARLIE** (*to the audience)* I decided to try my luck as New Talent tonight because, at my age, it's an accomplishment to appear as new anything. This is my first time. You'd never know it but I'm scared to death. I can't imagine why. What could be more natural than this, standing up in front of a room full of total strangers, attempting to give them the time of their lives? Actually, I'm accustomed to making a fool of myself. In real life, I'm the head writer for a soap opera. Many people ask me exactly what a head writer is. The fact is, the head writer is responsible for the characters only from the neck up. We have hand and foot writers, too. Even elbow writers if the script calls for a lot of nudging. People ask me how I can waste my talent writing for *Land of Dreams* — that's the name of the soap. What I tell them is, writing soap opera is a valuable community service. After a few afternoons watching Land of Dreams, even the chronically unemployed run out and get jobs. In case you're one of them, and wonder what's new on my show,

**CHARLIE** I'll tell you. Not much. Tommy's cystic fibrosis has flared up again; Sue's abortion didn't take. And Sarah's still hoping no one will notice that peculiar smell coming from the basement … Soap opera's what you call sit-down comedy. They told me the difference with stand-up was that the audience would rise if they liked a joke. So? … Does this mean I'm bombing? Too bad. I was planning to give up soap and get into this full-time. Not that TV hasn't been good to me. I live in a real classy part of town — the chic Carlton-Sherbourne area? Also known as the Heart of Darkness? You know, Yorkville Avenue has nothing on my neighbourhood …

*Blackout on* CHARLIE. *In the black, a tape of her voice takes over and continues the story. The taped voice is surer, brisker, more experienced, and there is audience laughter on the tape.*

**CHARLIE** (*on tape*) I mean, my neighbourhood has exclusive high-priced shops, too. They're called variety stores. In variety stores they look at you as though you're out of your mind if you ask for something really exotic — like a lemon. But they're great for staple items … If your idea of a staple item is a plaster-of-Paris cheetah. And say it's after six, and the other stores are closed and you run out of fluorescent yo-yos …

*Lights come up on the area that is* CHARLIE'S *apartment as the tape continues to run.* CHARLIE, *wearing her glasses, is slumped wearily in an armchair with a cigarette, a drink and a wrist-watch. She also has a notebook and a pen. To suggest that there has been progress in her stage "style" she wears a too-large suit jacket, a long aviator scarf, and a gaudy brooch or artificial flower. Her voice comes from a small cassette recorder on a nearby table.*

**CHARLIE** Still, you gotta watch those stores or they'll rip you off. I bought one of those litre-and-a-half bottles of Coke the other day? Damn thing refused to explode. It was a dud —

CHARLIE *snaps off the tape, scribbles a note to herself.*

**CHARLIE** (*spoken*) Fifteen-thirty. Too fucking long.

CHARLIE *looks down at the notations on the pad for a moment then loses interest, slumps back in the chair, sips her drink. Finally, after some indecision, she reaches for the phone, dials a long-distance number.*

**CHARLIE** (*into the phone*) Hi, sweetheart, I — (*pausing, then coldly*) Oh. Is Alan there? (*pausing*) That's right, it's Charlie. (*pausing*) Yes, I know it's you, Jackie. (*quickly*) Jimmy, I mean. Sorry, Jimmy. (*pausing*) Look, I said I was sorry. A simple mistake. Is Alan there? (*pausing*) Thank you so much. (*a longer pause, then her tone becomes warmer*) Hi, sweetheart. I just thought I'd call and — (*pausing*) Jimmy, right. Okay, okay, I won't get it wrong again. (*pausing*) Alan, I don't want to discuss my attitude. I'm lonesome and I need to talk to you. (*pausing*) Fine, have it your way. I'm lonesome and drinking and I need to talk to you. (*pausing*) Yeah, I'm still doing it. I was up tonight, in fact. Fifteenth triumphant performance at The Canada Goose. But I'm getting better. It would be nice if you'd come up to Toronto sometime and catch me. (*pausing, trying for lightness*) That's right, I work without a net. Look,

**CHARLIE** is there any chance of you coming to town? (*pausing, then with some asperity*) Uh huh. Well, when you have an audition here then. When it's worth your while to make the trip. (*pausing*) I know you didn't mean it that way, Alan. You never mean it that way. Look, I've got to get some sleep here. (*pausing*) Yeah, fine. Just fine. Don't worry. 'Bye, 'bye, sweetheart. Goodbye, Jackie. I can hear you breathing on the extension. (*slamming down the phone*) Fuck it.

CHARLIE *pours herself another drink, ponders a moment, then her expression relaxes and a sardonic smile crosses her face. She connects the mike to the tape recorder, pushes the record button.*

**CHARLIE** (*into the mike*) Jackie, Jimmy, what's the difference? I mean, they've all got names basically suitable for embroidering on the front of a pair of coveralls, right? Names they swiped off the Mouseketeers. Aw, but they're great guys, the Jackies and Jimmies and the Bobbies. I figure God invented gay guys so there'd be people around to remind us of how good the Bette Midler special was. If it weren't for gay guys, who'd buy bean-bag frogs? Or dimmer switches for the chandeliers? Most important, if there were no gay guys, who'd point out the smudged glasses in restaurants and send them back? Gay guys are terrific at sending back smudged glasses. It's weird, though. How they'll pick up some stranger at the baths, no questions asked, and end up on penicillin for six months. But they won't go near a smudged glass at Bemelmans. (*pausing, then wearily*) Take my life — please.

*Blackout.*

## Act One, Scene Two

*Lights come up on* GENE, *in shirt and jeans, sitting at a desk in the area that serves as his room. He speaks into the mike of a cassette recorder.*

GENE (*improvising) Deathless Prose*, by Eugene Bolton, is simply that. This daring, tough, tender, compassionate, evocative first novel by a breath-taking new talent makes Crime and Punishment look like a cakewalk; towers head and shoulders over anything Thomas Pynchon ever dreamed of writing, and would have killed Faulkner, were he not already dead. The young Canadian author … law student, bon vivant, and sometime employee of the Hudson's Bay Department Store —

*An alarm clock on the desk rings.* GENE *breaks off, shuts off the alarm and then the tape.*

GENE Shit. (*staring at the clock*) Now, what the hell? — Oh. (*leaning back, shouting*) Nick? Nick?

*No response.* GENE *puts on his glasses, rises, and leaves the desk area which is then plunged into blackness. As he moves into* NICK's *bedroom area, lights come up there to reveal an anonymous form asleep, alone in a large rumpled bed.* GENE *approaches the bed without really looking at the contents.*

**GENE** Come on, tiger. You order wake-up, you get wake-up. Ohh, say can you see, by the —

CHARLIE, *startled, sits up, clutching the sheet around her.*

**CHARLIE** What the fuck?

CHARLIE *and* GENE *stare at each other uncomprehendingly*

**GENE** Oh. Sorry. (*starting to leave)* As you were. As you were.

**CHARLIE** Wait!

CHARLIE *locates her glasses, puts them on, gazes around again but with no more comprehension.* GENE *watches as her glance falls on her own clothes, strewn on the floor.*

**GENE** (*kindly*) What's the matter? Don't you know where you are?

**CHARLIE** Of course I do. (*with a hopeful smile*) At your place.

**GENE** Lucky shot.

**CHARLIE** Don't be silly. I … (*infusion of warmth*) I had a wonderful time.

**GENE** Good. You must get it into your diary. Before it fades. (*as she continues to stare at him*) what's wrong?

**CHARLIE** You … look different, somehow.

**GENE** No way. I've looked the same since I was sixteen. I can show you my high school yearbook. (*sitting companionably on the bed*) Come on, admit it. You don't remember a goddamn thing.

**CHARLIE** I wish you wouldn't say that. (*rubbing her temples*) So loudly.

**GENE** Oldest feeling in the world. You have a couple too many, it feels like somebody slipped you a Mickey Finn. Strange guy brings you home, practises a little necrophilia on your comatose body. You wake up with a big headache and a big blank where your memory used to be …

**CHARLIE** You've got a great way with words. Have you considered cheap detective fiction?

**GENE** (*bleakly*) Right now I'm considering the monastery.

**CHARLIE** What?

**GENE** I might as well. I mean, usually a night with me is something a woman remembers all her life, tells her grandchildren about when they're old enough to hear … But look at the impression I made on you. El Blanko.

**CHARLIE** Bullshit. Total recall. It was great.

**GENE** Don't try to spare me. Besides, I wasn't too bowled over either.

**CHARLIE** Oh now, look, maybe the earth didn't pitch violently for either of us but you don't have to be like that.

**GENE** No, as far as I'm concerned, it never happened.

**CHARLIE** Of all the insulting … Look, we both made a mistake, that's all.

**GENE** (*grinning*) Uh-uh. *You* made a mistake, honey —

NICK *enters through the doorway, dressed only in slacks and socks, towelling his slightly damp hair.*

**GENE** Now, does this guy ring a bell?

**CHARLIE** (*glancing rapidly from* NICK *to* GENE) Why, you son of a bitch!

**NICK** (*mildly*) Hey, babe …

**CHARLIE** I mean him. (*indicating* GENE)

**GENE** You sure now? We all look alike in the dark.

**NICK** I see you two have met. (*kissing* CHARLIE) Hiya, babe.

**CHARLIE** (*faintly*) Hi.

**GENE** (*to* CHARLIE) His name is Nick.

**CHARLIE** (*quickly*) I know. Nick. I know.

**NICK** (*to* CHARLIE) Gene's my kid brother. But I guess you know that.

**CHARLIE** I didn't. But your awful secret's safe with me.

**NICK** (*laughing*) That's what you get, Geno. For sneaking in and trying to make time with my chick.

**GENE** You set your clock in my room. I assumed you wanted a wake-up.

**NICK** I did? Guess I was a little hammered last night.

**GENE** (*smiling at* CHARLIE) Lot of that going around.

**NICK** Anyway, I woke up early. And went down for a swim.

**CHARLIE** Swim?

**NICK** Yeah, this building has everything. Pool. Sauna. Squash.

**GENE** Elevators. The rent's eleven hundred a month. (*to* NICK) I thought I'd save you the trouble of telling her.

**NICK** Twelve hundred. Fuck off, little brother.

**GENE** And as a struggling student, I can only afford to give him one-seventy five. He'll tell you that, too.

**CHARLIE** Well, I'll try to act surprised.

**NICK** I said fuck off. There's coffee in the kitchen.

NICK *exits.*

**CHARLIE** Is he always like that?

**NICK** Just lately. He's working at The Bay for the summer. It gets him down. (*putting a robe around her shoulders*) He's going to make one sharp lawyer, though. Hey … (*warmly*) You were really good last night, babe. Did I tell you that?

**CHARLIE** (*pleased*) Thank you. You weren't so bad yourself.

**NICK** How do you think that stuff up?

**CHARLIE** Well … I just lie there, and it comes to me …

**NICK** Goddamn, that bit about lottery tickets —

**CHARLIE** Oh. The act.

**NICK** I'm telling you, you'd be great in a movie with that stuff.

**CHARLIE** Oh, come on, now …

**NICK** Seriously. You'd go. I've got an instinct for what goes. Every film I've put money in, I've made back at least double.

**CHARLIE** You're involved in movies?

**NICK** The financial end. And you'd go. But I told you that. Last night.

**CHARLIE** Nick, to tell you the truth, I'm just a little vague about last night. I mean, I guess we met at the club, and —

**NICK** You guess. You're cute. Christ, we sat there talking till they cleared all the glasses off the table — (*pausing*) You don't remember that? Jesus.

**CHARLIE** It's just … After a show, I — check out sometimes. Especially if I drink.

**NICK** Well, you certainly can drink. Hey, you were bombed? No, shit?

**CHARLIE** I wasn't bombed. Did I act bombed?

**NICK** No. Believe me, I'm not in the habit of dragging home drunken women.

**CHARLIE** And I wasn't drunk. I just have — gaps sometimes. My body keeps going after my mind

**CHARLIE** quits ... (*softly*) Hey, I remember some things. And I had a wonderful time.

**NICK** You sure now? I guess I could tell you it was the greatest sexual experience of your life and you'd have to believe me.

**CHARLIE** And how did it rate for you? (*quickly*) Forget it. It was a dumb question.

**NICK** Real dumb. (*kissing her*)

**CHARLIE** You have a certain backhand way with compliments.

**NICK** My forehand's pretty good too.

**CHARLIE** Well, sure. Squash courts right in the building.

**NICK** (*laughing*) You're great. Hey — (*kissing her*)

**CHARLIE** Hey what?

**NICK** Hey, where have you been all my life?

**CHARLIE** Waiting under the clock at Grand Central. What kept you?

**NICK** You want coffee or something?

**CHARLIE** (*seductively*) Something. If I have the choice.

**NICK** I'll get you some coffee.

**CHARLIE** (*disappointed*) Oh.

**NICK** It's just that I have a meeting this morning.

**CHARLIE** On Sunday? What are you, a Quaker?

**NICK** I have to see a man about a restaurant. That's my main weakness, restaurants. But I told you that.

**CHARLIE** This seems to have been a very open relationship. Too bad I missed it.

**NICK** What do you take in your coffee?

**CHARLIE** Cream and sugar. But I told you that.

**NICK** Smartass.

NICK *exits. Humming happily,* CHARLIE *locates her purse among the rubble of her clothing, takes a compact from it, looks at herself and abruptly stops humming. She starts scrubbing the smudged makeup on her face with a Kleenex.*

**CHARLIE** Jesus Christ. Gone for coffee, my ass. He's gone to call a plastic surgeon.

GENE *appears at the doorway with a mug of coffee.*

**GENE** You look ravishing.

**CHARLIE** (*turning in surprise*) Where's Nick?

**GENE** He's running late. Cream and sugar, right?

**CHARLIE** You mean he left?

**GENE** You know Nick. He hates emotional goodbyes. (*putting the coffee in her hand*) But he wanted you to have this. Don't worry, I'll drive you home.

**CHARLIE** You don't have to do that.

**GENE** Oh, I'm used to it.

**CHARLIE** What kind of crack is that — you're used to driving Nick's girls home?

**GENE** I don't want you to feel alone. As though you'd bombed somehow.

**CHARLIE** Thanks.

**GENE** Actually, I don't usually drive his girls.

**CHARLIE** Aha, I did bomb.

**GENE** No! It's just that most of them have cars.

**CHARLIE** I liked it better when I just felt alone. Gene, if you don't mind, I'd like to get dressed. Before you tell me how many other girls you've seen in this robe.

**GENE** Very few. It's mine.

**CHARLIE** Oh — I'm sorry.

**GENE** No sorrier than me. It looks good on you, though. That'll give me incentive.

**CHARLIE** Thank you. If you'll let me get dressed, you can have it back.

**GENE** You know, you shouldn't take Nick personally. He's got the manners of a forklift.

**CHARLIE** (*brightening*) You mean it was nothing I did?

**GENE** Boy, you really are something. You meet the guy — what, last night? And take the blame for the habits of a lifetime. (*as she says nothing*) Do you always assume everything's your fault?

**CHARLIE** I suppose this is a course in law school. Badgering the Witness.

**GENE** Law school's Nick's idea. Actually, I'm a writer.

**CHARLIE** Ah, you writers. Nothing much gets past you, does it? I'd really love to read your work. I think I've got an old sales slip from The Bay. Maybe it's one of yours?

**GENE** (*starting for the door*) The car's in the underground garage. Come down to the front door when you're dressed.

**CHARLIE** Gene! (*as he turns around*) I'm sorry. I make a lot of crummy jokes. Ask Nick. He saw my act.

**GENE** Nick liked your act. He told me.

**CHARLIE** Did he — mention anything else?

**GENE** (*smiling*) He'll call you. Sometime this evening.

**CHARLIE** You wouldn't kid me about that?

**GENE** No. I'm sorry I gave you such a hard time, when I woke you up.

**CHARLIE** Oh, what the hell … Talk to me when you're my age, sonny. We'll see if get all the names straight in the morning.

**GENE** Bullshit. You're the type who puts "Sleep Around" on her Things To Do list.

**CHARLIE** Now, what the hell is that supposed to mean?

**GENE** I just don't think you've got a lot of experience with this kind of thing. What are you, married or something? Divorced? Or — separated? Yeah, I like separated. Very half-assed. Very eighties.

**CHARLIE** Lucky shot.

**GENE** Naw, a lot of Nick's ladies are separated.

**CHARLIE** (*sinking down dispiritedly on the bed*) Just the ones without cars, I hope. I'd hate to fuck up the demographic profile.

**GENE** (*sitting down beside her*) I'm sorry. I really am.

**CHARLIE** So am I. About everything. Particularly the invention of alcohol.

**GENE** How much do you remember about last night?

**CHARLIE** Not much. Pretty funny, eh?

**GENE** I'm not laughing.

**CHARLIE** Neither am I. Say something hilarious.

**GENE** Want to get married?

**CHARLIE** (*with a startled laugh*) What?

**GENE** See? I knew that would raise a smile.

**CHARLIE** I can't marry a man with prospects. It's against my religion.

**GENE** I'm thinking of quitting law school.

**CHARLIE** Aw, that's what they all say.

**GENE** No, seriously, I am.

**CHARLIE** Even so, you can't marry me, sonny. I'm old enough to be your mother.

**GENE** Bullshit. You're only as old as you feel.

**CHARLIE** (*looking into her compact mirror wearily*) I know. Christ, look at this. First runner-up in the Rene Levesque Look-Alike Contest.

**GENE** Stop that. But I am going to quit. Don't tell Nick.

**CHARLIE** When am I going to tell him? I'll probably never see him again.

**GENE** Oh, you'll see him. If you want to.

**CHARLIE** You make it sound like I shouldn't.

**GENE** You make it sound like you want to. Get dressed and I'll drive you home.

**CHARLIE** I told you, I can get home myself.

**GENE** Okay. Whatever you like. (*moving to the door*)

**CHARLIE** Gene — (*as he stops*) Thanks — for the use of the robe.

**GENE** Anytime. I know — that's what they all say.

GENE *gives* CHARLIE *a smile and exits on a blackout.*

## Act One, Scene Three

*A couple of weeks later. Lights come up on the area that is* CHARLIE*'s apartment. The room is empty but there is the sound of someone rattling at the door. The rattling continues until a credit card slides through the lock, then the door opens and* ALAN *enters, with a small suitcase. He is obviously pleased with himself for pulling off the credit card stunt, shuts the door and tenderly replaces the card in his wallet. He puts down the suitcase, goes immediately to the phone and dials.*

**ALAN** (*into the phone*) Hello, Deborah? It's Alan. (*pausing*) Alan Merrit. The actor? One of your clients? (*laughing*) Right. That explains why you never get me any work. You have no idea who I am. (*pausing*) Yeah, slow season, I know. Funny how it's always slow season when I'm in town and Audition City when I'm away ... (*pausing*) Skip it, Deborah. I'll be in town a couple of days at — (*checking phone dial*) 967–1313. I'll check back with you before I leave. (*pausing*) Alan, that's right. Alan Merrit.

ALAN *hangs up dispiritedly, lights a cigarette, looks up an address in his book, then, dials again, singing quietly "I really want this job, I really need this job..."*

**ALAN** (*into the phone*) Hello, Grant Austin, please. It's Alan Merrit calling. (*pausing*) Hello, is he in? It's Alan Merrit. (*pausing*) Hello, Grant, it's ... (*pausing*) Oh. Well, could he come to the phone?

**ALAN** It's Alan Merrit. He's expecting my call. (*pausing*) Look, I made a special trip into town to see him. (*longer pause, then*) Grant! Hi! You said to call Tuesday and it's — (*pausing*) Alan Merrit? You said — (*pausing*) Alan, right. The actor? We met at the Moliere opening and ... (*pausing*) No, I wasn't exactly in it, but we talked at the bar after and — (*pausing*) Yeah, I guess I might have been in a red shirt. (*pausing*) Thank you, it's one of my favourite colours too ... Look, Grant, you said Tuesday would be a good day to call, so I came in from Stratford and — (*pausing*) Oh, next Tuesday. I guess I misunderstood. But I did come into town to see you, and — (*pausing*) Well, how be if I call back in the morning? Just to see if your schedule's cleared? I'd really like five minutes of your — (*pausing*) Okay, Grant, fine. I'll call back in the morning. (*hanging up, speaking bitterly to himself*) Any special colour you'd like me to wear?

*The phone, which is in his lap, rings. He starts violently, picks it up.*

**ALAN** Hello? (*pausing*) Look, I said not to call here. You know how she—(*pausing*) Yeah, I just got off the phone with Austin. He's delighted I'm here and wants to see me tomorrow. (*pausing*) Oh, it's not such a big deal. If you know the right strings to pull. (*pausing*) I don't know. Tomorrow night, maybe, or Thursday. Depends.

*Unnoticed by* ALAN, CHARLIE *has come in the open door and stands in the doorway. She has a paper bag of liquor in her arms.*

**ALAN** (*into the phone*) Yes, I miss you, too. But I —

*As* CHARLIE *rattles the bag angrily,* ALAN *turns and sees her.*

**ALAN** (*into the phone*) Look, I've got to go, okay? Call you tomorrow. (*hanging up, turning to* CHARLIE *with a bright smile*) Hiya, babe!

**CHARLIE** Well, surprise, surprise! (*allowing* ALAN *to kiss her*) Who was that on the phone?

**ALAN** Nobody. Casting people.

**CHARLIE** Who misses you? Shucks, I bet they say that to all the actors. It was him, wasn't it?

**ALAN** He's got a name, you know.

**CHARLIE** "Casting people." Why do you keep lying — force of habit?

**ALAN** I just got here. Can't we save the cracks for later?

**CHARLIE** How'd you get in?

**ALAN** Credit card.

**CHARLIE** That's amazing.

**ALAN** (*self-effacing*) Oh, I wouldn't go that far …

**CHARLIE** That you were actually issued a credit card? That's nothing short of miraculous.

**ALAN** Actually, it's Jimmy's.

**CHARLIE** Good old Jimmy. Say it with plastic. So what are you doing in town?

**ALAN** You've been after me to come up and see you.

**CHARLIE** Uh-huh. And — ?

**ALAN** And … I've got some people to see.

**CHARLIE** Yeah, I figured.

**ALAN** Grant Austin, for one. I hope that's okay.

**CHARLIE** Well, if it's okay with Grant Austin, it's okay with me.

**ALAN** I mean, it's all right to stay here.

**CHARLIE** Here? In my apartment? It's out of the question.

**ALAN** Charlie, I'm your husband. Who's going to object?

**CHARLIE** My boyfriend, to name one.

**ALAN** I didn't know you had a steady boyfriend,

**CHARLIE** I figured if you had one, I should too. Alan, Nick will be here in a minute. We're going to The Canada Goose.

**ALAN** You're on tonight? Terrific. Can I join you?

**CHARLIE** You want to come along? You won't feel a little weird about Nick?

**ALAN** Should I? I mean, is there something organically wrong with him?

**CHARLIE** I give up. You can't crash here. That's all there is to it.

**ALAN** That's nice. That's very nice. After eight years of marriage, this is what I get?

**CHARLIE** (*quiz show voice*) This, Alan, and much more! During your marriage, you received: four million loads of clean laundry; the keys to a car your wife never got to drive; leftovers no more than twice a week; plus sex available at several convenient

**CHARLIE** locations in your own home! ! Yes, Alan, these are only some of the prizes you won playing Eight Years of Marriage!

**ALAN** Charlie, don't be that way. I thought we'd got past all the bitterness.

**CHARLIE** I hope not. I mean, when that's gone, what's left?

**ALAN** I don't know. A new start maybe?

**CHARLIE** As what? I admit, I've always wanted a sister, but ...

**ALAN** Knock that off.

**CHARLIE** Then you knock it off. (*pouring herself a drink*) Oh, Alan, don't tell me you're having doubts about your femininity again.

**ALAN** I should know better than to expect to be taken seriously.

**CHARLIE** Oh, I took you seriously, all right. The last two years of our marriage when you said you were working late all those nights. I took you seriously when you told me I was crazy to think any different. And I took you very seriously indeed when you disappeared into the pages of Christopher Street never to emerge again. Now, I'd say there was a limit to just how long a person can go on taking you seriously. Or any way at all. Wouldn't you?

**ALAN** If that's how you feel, why do you keep asking me to come and see you?

**CHARLIE** I don't know.

**ALAN** Neither do I. Can you pour me one too?

| | |
|---|---|
| **CHARLIE** | On one condition. That you refrain from referring to homosexuality as a "phase." You always make it sound like teenage acne. (*giving him a drink*) |
| **ALAN** | I know what you've been through. But it's not easy on me, either. Especially when you phone me up, late at night — |
| **CHARLIE** | There won't be any more calls. Not that kind. I'm feeling much better now. |
| **ALAN** | Thanks to Nick? |
| **CHARLIE** | What's the matter? Don't you believe someone could be interested in me? |
| **ALAN** | Oh, I believe it. Do you? |
| **CHARLIE** | I don't have this adverse effect on everybody, you know. I don't drive all men to gay bars. |
| **ALAN** | Did I ever say you did? |
| **CHARLIE** | Yes. |
| **ALAN** | (*after a pause*) I'm sorry. I guess I had to blame somebody. |
| **CHARLIE** | I wish you'd picked your mother, like everybody else. She lives six hundred miles away. It wouldn't have fucked her up. |
| **ALAN** | You're not fucked up. Not any more. Thanks to Nick. |
| **CHARLIE** | So it does bother you a little? |
| **ALAN** | We've been split up almost a year. I know there've been guys ... |

**CHARLIE** Oh dear, and I thought I was so discreet!

**ALAN** Come on. You always made sure I knew.

**CHARLIE** (*after a pause*) Most of those guys were clunkers.

**ALAN** And Nick isn't a clunker? (*pausing*) Okay, it bothers me.

**CHARLIE** (*gently*) It's just this phobia you've got. About closed doors. Most people think of the world as their oyster. In your mind, it's one big telephone exchange. With everyone on hold.

**ALAN** Only you, babe. Come here, and let me put you on hold. (*hugging her*)

*There is a knock on the door.*

**CHARLIE** That's Nick. I guess he forgot his credit card.

CHARLIE *opens the door.* NICK *enters, gives her a bottle of champagne.*

**NICK** Hiya, babe. Bubbly to the bubbly. In honour of your performance.

**CHARLIE** I perform twice a week. Champagne is for special.

**NICK** Then be specially good. Dom Perignon, kid. Don't give me no domestic-bubbly performance. (*kissing her, then sees* ALAN) Oh. Hi.

**CHARLIE** Nick, this is Alan. (*as the men shake hands*) My late husband.

**NICK** (*dropping the hand like a hot rock*) Charlie! Jesus.

**ALAN** Charlie's little joke. And it's little.

**NICK** (*backing toward the door*) Look, I didn't know you were double-booked here. And if you two have things to straighten out—

**CHARLIE** (*quickly*) No, Alan's just dropped in from Stratford.

**ALAN** (*also quick*) Just to say hello.

**CHARLIE** (*even quicker*) Not even that, practically.

**ALAN** Don't mind me.

**NICK** (*shrugging sheepishly*) If you'd had as many husbands sprung on you as I have ... Now, whenever I hear the word, I automatically check the exits. (*to* ALAN) In from Stratford, eh?

**ALAN** Couple of business things.

**NICK** Ball bearings?

**ALAN** I beg your pardon?

**NICK** (*innocently*) That's what they do up in Stratford, isn't it?

**CHARLIE** Nick's little joke. He grew up there. He knows goddamn well there's a theatre there.

**NICK** She's right. Saturday nights, our idea of a hot old time was driving into town to bash a few faggot actors.

**CHARLIE** (*quickly*) Have a drink, Nick. (*producing a bottle from the bag*) I got some Scotch, just for you. Alan?

**ALAN** (*campily*) No thanks. I'll stick to Shirley Temples.

**NICK** (*laughing*) Hey, that's good. So, you're with the Festival. Watch your ass, that's all I can say.

**ALAN** (*very macho*) I'm not with the Festival yet. You think I'm watching my ass too closely?

**NICK** Could be. What do you think, Charlie? You're the resident expert on the gay scene.

**ALAN** (*to* CHARLIE) Do tell.

**NICK** Babe, how does that bit go, about the faggots in the restaurant? (*to* ALAN) They're always sending back dirty forks, right, then they pick up some stranger and get the clap.

**ALAN** That's very funny, Charlie. Not very insightful, but funny.

**CHARLIE** I do a whole bunch of different stuff. You'll see.

**ALAN** Some other time, maybe.

**CHARLIE** I thought you wanted to come tonight.

**ALAN** I've changed my mind. (*picking up his suitcase*) Have a good show. I'll call you tomorrow.

**CHARLIE** Alan —

**ALAN** (*more conciliatory*) Look, I've got a heavy day tomorrow. I have to be on the phone early to Grant Austin and —

**NICK** Grant? You working with him?

**ALAN** (*stiffly*) I'd like to.

**NICK** (*to* CHARLIE) Grant was on that picture I told you about. Christ, I more than tripled on that one.

**ALAN** (*setting down his suitcase*) Lupercal? You have money in that?

**NICK** Lucky me. You see the numbers on that fucker?

**ALAN** No, but I saw the fucker. It was great.

**NICK** Grant's dynamite. Camp as a row of tents but a hell of a director. You seeing him tomorrow?

**ALAN** He's not sure what his time is like.

**NICK** Well, he starts casting next week. You better catch him before the big rush.

**ALAN** You don't happen to know what the film is?

**NICK** Another blockbuster, I hope. I've got money in this one, too.

**ALAN** (*avidly*) No kidding? You haven't seen a script, by any chance?

**NICK** I know where to get one. Why?

**ALAN** (*to* CHARLIE) Listen, maybe I can join you at the club. Once I dump the suitcase …

**CHARLIE** I thought you had such an early day ahead.

**ALAN** (*artificially sweet*) I thought you wanted me to see your act.

**CHARLIE** (*the same*) A minute ago, my act rated slightly below trench-mouth.

**ALAN** I haven't got any idea what you're talking about.

**CHARLIE** Haven't you? I mean it's just amazing how the atmosphere in this room has warmed up since Grant Austin dropped in.

**ALAN** (*to* NICK) You don't mind if I join you later at The Canada Goose? And maybe talk about this new script?

**NICK** I don't mind. I like to talk. Charlie knows that.

**ALAN** (*picking up his suitcase*) See you later, then. 'Bye, babe.

ALAN *exits.* CHARLIE *takes a long sip of her drink*

**NICK** Nervous kind of guy. He any good?

**CHARLIE** I don't know. He never gives himself a chance to find out. He's too busy making useful contacts.

**NICK** You should talk. Soon as you found out I backed movies, you couldn't get your clothes off fast enough.

**CHARLIE** Nick! You don't believe that.

**NICK** Come on, you're entitled to your self-interest, like everybody else. It doesn't detract from the quality of the sex.

**CHARLIE** I'm telling you, I'm not in it for the fringe benefits. I want to get that clear, Nick.

**NICK** You people with "pure motives." You make me nervous.

**CHARLIE** Oh, I'm not so pure … (*putting her arms around him*) Let's not talk about work. You've already got

**CHARLIE** Alan prepared to lay down his life for you because you might be useful to him. Isn't that enough?

**NICK** I don't get it. If I can get him in to see Austin, why shouldn't I? If I can do you a favour, why not? What is it? You've got your life in ledger columns? "Business." "Romance."

**CHARLIE** That's right. Just don't mix me in with business, that's all. This town is one giant office. Casting done in bars. Contracts ratified on waterbeds. People sucking up to power because it might rub off. Those macrobiotic people had it all wrong. Around here, you are who you eat.

**NICK** You don't know a goddamn thing about it. Work, sex, dinner, dealing — it's all the same. I don't even try keeping them apart. And I like people who do the same. No questions asked.

**CHARLIE** (*pouring herself a drink*) That's a tall order.

**NICK** (*indicating drink*) Hey, you're working tonight. Were you always such a little lush? Even when you were married to what's-his-name?

**CHARLIE** Lush. You make me sound like a golf course. This is only my second. And anyway, what's it got to do with what's-his-name?

**NICK** That's what I wonder. What broke you two up? You never told me.

**CHARLIE** You never asked. I like that arrangement. (*kissing him*) I don't want to talk about it. I want to fool around.

**NICK** You always want to fool around. What did you do, wear the guy out?

**CHARLIE** (*sharply*) Will you forget about Alan?

**NICK** No, I want to know. What was the problem?

**CHARLIE** (*exasperated*) Isn't it obvious? My frigidity!

**NICK** Hey. How come you always act like you'll never get laid again?

**CHARLIE** Right now, I'd settle for a really decisive kiss.

NICK *sighs, then kisses her very decisively.* CHARLIE *pulls away finally, hesitates for a moment before speaking.*

**CHARLIE** Nick ... Do you think I'm attractive?

**NICK** You haven't figured that out?

**CHARLIE** I mean — do you like being with me?

**NICK** Hell, no. When you stop giving green stamps, I'm gone.

**CHARLIE** (*urgently*) Nick — please?

**NICK** (*pausing, then with slight distaste*) Okay. Of course I like being with you. Very much.

**CHARLIE** Yeah, I figured. (*pulling him to her, kissing him*)

**NICK** Hardcore comes later. It's almost show time.

**CHARLIE** How be if I skip the club? We could have a nice evening — just you, me and Dom Perignon.

**NICK** You can't just back out.

**CHARLIE** Sure I can. There's always someone hanging around who'll take over my spot.

**NICK** You expect to get ahead with an attitude like that?

**CHARLIE** It was just a thought.

**NICK** What's the problem?

**CHARLIE** I just don't feel very funny tonight.

**NICK** No? Well, you goddamn well better be. Unless you want to sleep alone.

**CHARLIE** (*mock terror*) Oh, shit. (*quickly*) Say, did I ever tell you the one about the lady comic, her bullying boyfriend and the vat of cold vichyssoise? Funny? You bet. Seems the comic was walking over the vichyssoise on a tightrope and —

**NICK** Okay, okay. You don't sleep alone. Now let's get the fuck out of here.

CHARLIE *picks up her purse and* NICK *slaps her on the ass on the way out the door on a blackout.*

## Act One, Scene Four

*Later that night. Lights come up on The Canada Goose.* CHARLIE *wears the now habitual uniform of her performance her glasses, jacket, scarf, and brooch.*

**CHARLIE** (*bounding down to the mike, removing it from stand, addressing the audience*) Hi, how is everybody tonight? Come on, it's not a trick question. How about you, sir? How are you? (*if an audience member doesn't answer*) It's all right, sir. I read lips. (*if audience member does answer*) Who asked you?

Hey, I'm in a great mood tonight. I just got my Mensa card. (*taking a card from her pocket, showing it*) You know what that means? It means I'm insured against ever skipping a period. So … how do you like my hair? Mr. Doug did it. That's my hairdresser — Mr. Doug. Ever notice what flamboyant names Canadian hairdressers have? Mr. Doug. Mr. Glen. Mr. Garth of North Bay. Mr. Doug told me he was just going to "shape the hair." Notice how they never refer to it as YOUR hair? This is so they can wreck it without either of you feeling personally affected by it.

But I trust Mr. Doug. Implicitly. I mean, he doesn't charge an arm and a leg like those trendy uptown places where you pay for the decor and the cute little cover-up robe. Mr. Doug works out of an auto body shop. He keeps his costs down that way. Although I notice the Turtle Wax IS doing strange things to my hair. And there was this mix-up one day where a lady came in for a cut and

**CHARLIE** set and wound up getting a ring job. (*to an audience member who is laughing*) Hey, that's not funny. It's tragic. I suppose you laughed when Ben Hur's mother and sister got leprosy.

You know, I have what people in showbusiness describe as a great RADIO face. Actually, it's not mine. It comes attached to the glasses. It's part of a disguise. See, when you look like Bo Derek, everybody mobs you. Okay, okay … so I don't look like Bo Derek. But I am a Ten. I'm what they call a Canadian Ten. Which means they don't even accept me at par in Buffalo. (*indicating audience member*) This man is laughing. He has no idea what I go through. Great shirt, sir. How long do you have to wear it before you win the bet?

Oh, by the way, a note was slipped to me backstage. But I intend to go on with the act anyway. No, seriously … I have a note here. (*producing note from her pocket, reading from it*) Mrs D. of Erin Mills writes: "Dear Charlie, where do you get your ideas for the characters on *Land of Dreams?*" Oh, in case you don't know, *Land of Dreams* is the name of this soap opera I write for. Where do I get my ideas for characters, Mrs D.? I steal them from American soaps and change their names to Glen and Doug. Any more questions? (*without waiting for a reply*) Fine.

Hey, you know, I always wanted to be one of those teensy little girls. You know the kind I mean? The kind of girl whose nickname is Bitsy? The kind of girl I lend a bracelet to and she wears it as a belt. Helpless. That was always my goal in life. To be helpless. Helpless and sweet and quiet. Like Bitsy. Bitsy never has to talk. She's mastered one simple basic sentence — "How was your day, honey?" — and the world's beating a path to her door. I meanwhile am lucky if a guy ventures up

**CHARLIE** my walk to read my meter. See, men just don't come on to big, capable girls — girls who speak English as if it was their native language. Especially when your voice sounds like Full Alert in the London Blitz. I ask a guy if he wants to come to bed, and it sounds like a threat.

Now, Bitsy has this tiny, feminine, whispering voice, right? Put her on a phone, man, and she gets results. (*imitating*) "Hello? Oh, hi, Brad. Dinner? No thanks. I just ate half a soda biscuit and I couldn't touch another thing."

And when Bitsy goes shopping for clothes, the clerks always advise her to try the Petite Section, right? The Petite Section. It even sounds elegant, doesn't it? So what do they call the large section? You guessed it. The Large Section. And I so much as even try walking into the Petite Section and they throw a cordon around the entire department and get on the bullhorns (*imitating*) "Attention all staff. Large person attempting entry. Large person attempting entry." Then they send some little Munchkin over to reason with me, right? (*imitating*) "Listen, honey, nothing personal, but you're built like a Maytag, all right?"

You notice how tiny all the clerks are in the Petite Section? The manager of the department wears a point-zero-six dress. I'm not kidding. And when I won't go quietly, the entire staff rushes to the barricades. It looks like a convention of jockeys. They all swarm around my kneecaps chanting — (*imitates*) "Follow the yellow brick road. Follow the yellow brick road … "

Hey, you've been a great audience. Thank you and good night!

*Blackout.*

## Act One, Scene Five

*Later that night. Lights come up on a table in The Canada Goose where* ALAN *sits alone with a full drink on the table.* CHARLIE, *dressed as in Scene Four, hurries breathlessly to the table. She stops short, glances around.*

ALAN (*rising, kissing her*) Babe, that was dynamite.

CHARLIE Where's Nick?

ALAN He said he's sorry he missed the act. Something —

CHARLIE (*joining in*) "Something came up." Fuck. (*sitting down*)

ALAN He went to make a call about that script and when he came back he said he had to leave.

CHARLIE You had to have that goddamn script, didn't you?

ALAN Since you asked, yes. It would be very helpful. (*pausing*) He said he'd try to make it back to your place later.

CHARLIE White of him. I want a drink.

ALAN (*pushing the drink over to her*) Here — ordered it for you.

CHARLIE Thanks.

ALAN Babe, you were wonderful. The fact that Nick missed it doesn't change that.

**CHARLIE** You think that's all I care about? Whether he saw the fucking act?

**ALAN** I figured you'd care. Nick says he'd like to back a film with you in it.

**CHARLIE** I'm not in it to get ahead! I don't quaff cocktails with people I hate just to get a script.

**ALAN** Is that how you think I operate?

**CHARLIE** I watched you operate with Nick.

**ALAN** (*bitterly*) All right, so what? The guy's a redneck but his money's the same colour as anyone else's. If Grant Austin can put up with Nick's faggot jokes, I guess I can too. (*pausing*) You don't understand, Charlie. You can stand up in front of a roomful of people without anybody's help and run your own show. I can't.

**CHARLIE** Oh, I know how to get love from groups of twenty or more, all right. But one to one? You could give me some tips in that area. I mean, at least you've got Jackie —

**ALAN** (*mechanically*) Jimmy —

**CHARLIE** — Jimmy, to keep the home fires burning while you're out knocking on doors. I come out of the spotlight and find the bastard's taken a powder.

**ALAN** Charlie, it's not easy. For anybody. But as long as you've got the spotlight, you're way ahead. I wish I could do what you do — dress up in a costume and act out my worst fears about myself.

**CHARLIE** It's not a costume!

**ALAN** Come on. You look like an out-take from Annie Hall. All the years I knew you, you were too vain to wear your glasses, even.

**CHARLIE** (*snatching off her glasses*) There are no glamorous lady comics. It doesn't work.

**ALAN** You dress like that because you think it's how you really look. I admire you for that. I wouldn't have the nerve to go up there — or anywhere else — and try to be myself.

**CHARLIE** (*taking his hand*) Sweetheart, what's the matter?

**ALAN** It's — confusing, that's all. I think I've got my priorities straight — or bent, or something. Then I see you, and you're telling stories about queers, picking up tricks.

**CHARLIE** (*quickly*) I didn't use any of that stuff tonight.

**ALAN** But you tell the stories all the same. And I don't recognize myself in them.

**CHARLIE** Of course not. Alan, that isn't you.

**ALAN** Then what is? What do you see, Charlie?

**CHARLIE** I don't know. What do you want me to see? What do you want me to do?

**ALAN** I don't know. I had some idea, when I decided to come into town that maybe … (*shrugging*)

**CHARLIE** That maybe what?

**ALAN** Of course, I didn't know about Nick. I hadn't counted on that.

**CHARLIE** (*urgently*) Alan, you can't do this to me. If you want something, tell me.

**ALAN** I guess there's nothing you can do.

**CHARLIE** Not if you're going to be so goddamn cryptic.

**ALAN** Charlie, what difference does it make now? Nick's in the picture and all bets are off.

**CHARLIE** You mean it's safe to make overtures, now that I'm hooked on someone else?

**ALAN** Yeah. I guess maybe that's it. You are hooked, aren't you?

**CHARLIE** Yes, I'm afraid so.

**ALAN** That's all right, then.

**CHARLIE** Not from where I sit. God, I wish I knew how he felt about me.

**ALAN** And if the verdict's favourable? You might decide you're fit to live?

**CHARLIE** Isn't that what it means when you're hooked?

**ALAN** No! There's a big difference between caring about him and building your life around the idea. I mean, when do you stop expecting other people to supply you with self-respect?

**CHARLIE** You make me sound like a backward nation. (*travelogue voice*) "Here in Charlieland, the natives try to find enough self-esteem to power even one generator."

**ALAN** That's not funny, babe.

**CHARLIE** Neither is venereal disease. But you know, it's a sure-fire laugh?

*Blackout.*

## Act One, Scene Six

*A few days later. Lights come up in* NICK*'s bedroom.* NICK *is asleep.* GENE *comes in, begins stealthily dialing the phone.* NICK *stirs, raises his head.*

**NICK** (*annoyed and sleepily*) What? Gene, what the fuck are you doing?

**GENE** (*hanging up the phone*) Sorry, but the one in the kitchen is temporarily out of service.

**NICK** (*rubbing his eyes*) This is just an extension, you asshole. It won't work either.

**GENE** Sure it will. It's out of the war zone. Mustard gas attack in the kitchen. (*German accent*) It's dat Sharlie again, mein Kapitan. She shtrikes mitout varning.

**NICK** Charlie? (*looks at the empty side of the bed*) What's she doing up?

**GENE** Cleaning the fridge.

**NICK** Oh fuck. This is too much. Yesterday she made blueberry pancakes.

**GENE** Last week she washed the windows.

**NICK** Next thing I'll wake up to find my goddamn room re-papered.

**GENE** I think you should nip this thing in the bud. Remember your stewardess? Almost six feet of

**GENE** stunning blonde stooped over the bathtub, scouring away with Spic and Span?

**NICK** If that's how you feel, why don't you tell Charlie to knock it off?

**GENE** Because it's not my fault she thinks the way to your heart is through your stinking refrigerator. Nick you owe it to her to straighten her out.

**NICK** No way. A woman's determined to dig her own grave, I'm not going to hide the shovel.

**GENE** Christ. Maybe you should just tell her you don't have a heart.

**NICK** Come on, it's too early in the morning for that crap.

**GENE** It's eleven-thirty and there's a woman in the kitchen humming, if you'll believe it, while she dungs rotted matter out of the fridge whose stench would turn the stomach of a wart hog. Christ, there are carrots covered in blue fuzz and mutated leftovers that the Special Effects Department at Universal should only take a look at. And yet she is out there humming, Nick — I swear it's God's honest truth — because those noxious vapours emanate from your fridge, your kitchen, your apartment, and, as far as she's concerned, anything that pertains to you is strictly Chanel Number Five. No, I don't think it's at all too early in the morning for that crap. And either you go out there and tell her you love what's she doing or advise her she's spelling out her own destruction in moulded spuds. But either way, wear a gas mask, I'm warning you.

**NICK** I don't need advice on women from you. I wrote the book.

**GENE** I know. It's the one with the large print and the small words. You won't help her, will you? You won't help her at all.

**NICK** All this sudden concern for Charlie. What's the matter, you fumble the ball with that great-looking cocktail waitress? Sure you did, I can tell. I fix you up on Saturday night and here you are on Sunday morning, all by yourself. Unless Donna is out in the kitchen battling bacteria with good old Charlie.

**GENE** Donna would be better off if she were into fridges. Something. Anything. What do you talk about to someone whose idea of a moral dilemma is whether hot pink clashes with green?

**NICK** You took Donna out to *talk?*

**GENE** I had it in mind as an option.

**NICK** Christ, what am I going to do with you? I fix you up with a beautiful girl who borders on genius, sexually speaking, and you complain because she isn't a Rhodes scholar in the bargain. What is it, they haven't invented a woman good enough for you?

**GENE** Once in my life, I'd like a shot at a woman you haven't slept with first. Although I realize such women are hard to find.

**NICK** Too bad you feel that way. Otherwise, you could take Charlie off my hands.

**GENE** Oh, sure, we'd both go for that. I mean, her glasses are almost as strong as mine. Lasting relationships have been based on less. (*with distaste*) Nick, Jesus Christ …

**NICK** You're right, it's not much of a thought. She's cute, but she's nutty as a fruitcake. And she acts like she's mainlining Spanish Fly.

**GENE** That doesn't sound so bad.

**NICK** Don't kid yourself. That woman doesn't just like to screw. She needs it. Like a drug.

**GENE** Like a drug, eh? Wow. Of course, you're in your thirties. I keep forgetting. No longer the ideal … drug pusher?

**NICK** You know who puts out that crap — about men beginning to decline at age nineteen? Hostile women put it out, that's who. It's all part of a plot to discredit us. (*pausing*) Anyway, Charlie's way too old for you.

**GENE** I'm twenty-three.

**NICK** And she's thirty. That's exactly what I mean.

**GENE** No, that's exactly what I mean. Charlie and I would be the ideal combination.

**NICK** Bullshit. Sexual peaks have nothing to do with Charlie.

**GENE** I wonder. I mean, here you are, so impressed with Donna's sexual prowess. A younger woman, not yet in her prime, not so difficult to keep up with …

**NICK** Good, Geno, you're doing fine. You'll be looking for a new apartment by lunchtime.

**GENE** Hey, Nick, for Christ's sake. I'm only kidding.

**NICK** (*sulkily*) I'm telling you, that stuff about peaks is crap. I'm as hot as I ever was. With the right woman.

**GENE** You mean you really don't want Charlie any more?

**NICK** For Christ's sake, I just woke up. How the hell do I know what I want? I want to be a millionaire before I'm forty, I want a cup of coffee. I want a woman for a change who doesn't turn into Betty Crocker on a moment's notice.

**GENE** So what are you going to do? Order the perfect one out of the catalogue? Relationships have to be worked on, haven't you heard?

**NICK** I work hard all day long. Why should I work when I come home, too? Either it clicks with a woman or it doesn't and all the heart-to-heart talks in the world never fixed anything. Take it from Nicky. Nicky knows. Gene, on the other hand, knows zip.

**GENE** (*quietly*) Poor Charlie.

**NICK** Will you cut it out? Anyway, it's not like we're a couple or anything.

**GENE** What would you call it? A string quartet?

**NICK** It was just for — fun, that's all. But when the fun goes ... Well, I just don't have that much enthusiasm for it any more.

**GENE** Big brother, you haven't had much enthusiasm for anybody since about nineteen-sixty-eight. Since then, it's been painting by numbers.

**NICK** You know, this interest you take in my relationships is downright unhealthy. Why don't

**NICK** you find a project of your own — like losing your virginity?

**GENE** You think anybody whose little black book comes in fewer volumes than the Britannica is a virgin. I've been around. But unlike you, I can remember where.

**NICK** Yeah? When was the last time you got laid? I mean, here you are, so hot to be a writer. What the hell are you going to write about?

**GENE** If you're still pissed off about law school, why don't you just admit it?

**NICK** Me, pissed off? Hell, no. Why, I've got the First Lady of Show Business into some heavy defrosting out in my kitchen. And in the bedroom, the kid I staked through two years of law school who's decided on a permanent career at the pen counter of The Bay instead. By God, I'm a lucky son of a gun. I think my life would make great musical comedy, don't you?

**GENE** I'm sorry, I'm just not cut out for law school. Besides, I won't be at The Bay forever. Look at Charlie. She makes a living writing.

**NICK** Charlie! Is she the inspiration behind this? God, it was a dark day when I let her and her arsenal of cleaning products in here.

**GENE** Don't be so melodramatic. It was my own idea.

**NICK** Yeah? Well, at least you're right about one thing. If you're going to be a writer, make a full-time career out of it. I know people who'd be interested in you.

**GENE** I don't think I want to write menus.

**NICK** Not restaurant people, you asshole. Movie people.

**GENE** I've got to do it my way. Me and Sinatra.

**NICK** First you let somebody get you in the door. Then you do it your way.

**GENE** Nick, it's bad enough I live here at Club Med with you and pay one-seventy-five in rent. I'm not going to use your connections too.

**NICK** You're my brother. I feel responsible.

**GENE** (*Italian accent*) Eh, Niccolo, listen to your brother, eh? Alla time, you give, give, give. But never nothing outa yourself. Capisce?

**NICK** Jesus, it's as bad as talking to Charlie. Worse.

**GENE** All my life — fastest cheque book in the West, favours done while you wait. And champagne always on ice.

**NICK** I never bought anybody in my life.

**GENE** I've seen you buy a few people off. Tell me, when Charlie gets her pink slip, will she get the bouquet of roses that traditionally goes with it?

**NICK** Jesus, I wish you'd get off that. Or go after her yourself, if you're so concerned.

**GENE** And break Jane Fonda's heart?

**NICK** (*grinning*) Don't lie to me, you little fucker. You'd do it, wouldn't you? You'd do it just for spite.

**GENE** Not for spite. But maybe to jazz up her sex life a little.

**NICK** (*laughing*) Get the fuck out of my room. And don't touch my phone either. (*as* GENE *goes*) You little wise-ass, you're twenty-three years old and a law school drop-out. (*wearily*) And I'm a hundred and twelve. Easy.

*Blackout.*

**Act One, Scene Seven**

*Two days later. Lights come up on* CHARLIE *on the phone in her apartment, There are a couple of empty wine bottles beside her and she has a glass in her hand. She is drunk but not inarticulate. A bouquet of roses is bundled conspicuously in a wastebasket.*

**CHARLIE** (*into the phone*) No, I'm not drinking. Alan, you sound like my mother, except your voice is higher. (*quickly*) I'm sorry, I didn't mean that. Don't hang up, please. (*pausing*) I know there weren't going to be any more calls but this is important. Maybe I've been too categorical about things. Maybe we could get back together someday. Stranger things have happened, right? And until everything went crazy, we were happy together. (*pausing, then firmly*) Goddamn it, we were, until you took this notion to emulate the late Oscar Wilde. I think it's a fad, Alan, just a trendy fad. In the sixties, everybody went back to the land. In the seventies, they went gay. And in the eighties — (*pausing, then wearily*) I know. I still love you, too. But we sure have a funny way of showing it. (*pausing*) Yes, okay, I'm drinking. Maybe I'm drunk. (*pausing*) I don't know why. See, there was this bottle here and I — (*pausing, then bitterly*) No, Nick is not here. (*beginning to cry*) How the hell do I know where Nick is? (*listening into the phone, nodding corroboration, and, when she can manage it, speaking*) Yes, finished. As far as I knew, everything was going fine. Then today I get the kiss-off, and tonight these roses arrive. He sends roses and a note that Kahlil Gibran must

**CHARLIE** have ghosted. "No regrets. No bitterness. No blame." what the hell does that mean? After all this, he buys me off with cryptic platitudes. And a lunch. I knew there was going to be trouble when he asked me to lunch. Never, never go to lunch. It's always the bad-news meal. Everytime I — (*pausing*) Nick has nothing to do with this call. I told you, I love you. And you said that you — (*pausing, then angrily*) Wait and see? How the hell do you expect me to wait and see? You were a beautiful boy when I met you and now you're nothing but a goddamn — faggot! (*pausing*) I can't get past it. Can you get past it? Eight goddamn years, Alan. How the hell do I get that back? There's just nowhere to go from here. (*pausing*) I don't know what I mean by that!

CHARLIE *slams down the phone and pulls the jack out of the wall on a blackout.*

## Act One, Scene Eight

*A few hours later. Lights up in* CHARLIE'*s apartment. The scene is unchanged except for an added empty bottle or two.* CHARLIE *sits on the bed, more sober, singing into the mike on her tape recorder.*

CHARLIE

When the tires are humming,
And the engine purrs,
And your car is eager,
And the thought occurs:
It's good to be alive in this land of ours,
It's good to drive in this land of ours —

*Unnoticed by* CHARLIE, GENE *has entered, and, as* CHARLIE *falters, he sings the next line of the song.*

GENE

What a great, great feeling,
What a wonderful sense —

CHARLIE, *with no hint of surprise, turns to him and they continue the song together, building to a strong and zesty finale*

GENE & CHARLIE

Of sheer enjoyment,
And of confidence.
There's something you're aware of,
Your car's been taken care of,
At the Esso sign of confidence,

**GENE & CHARLIE** At the Happy Motoring Sign!

CHARLIE *and* GENE *salute each other simultaneously and bark "Happy Motoring' Murray Westgate-style, then laugh uproariously.*

**CHARLIE** How do you know that? You weren't even born back then.

**GENE** Don't you believe in the collective unconscious?

**CHARLIE** Oh sure. It's the collective conscious I have doubts about.

**GENE** Aren't you going to ask me how I got in?

**CHARLIE** Visa, American Express — what's the difference?

**GENE** The door's open, that's how. Charlie, it's late. Don't you ever lock it?

**CHARLIE** Is that what brings you here? A survey on the Imprudent Habits of Single Women?

**GENE** They missed you down at The Canada Goose tonight.

**CHARLIE** What were you doing at the club?

**GENE** I knew you were on tonight.

**CHARLIE** Yeah? How did I do? (*laughing, but he doesn't join in*)

**GENE** When I got there, Mel was trying to get you on the phone to find out where the hell you were. (*going to the phone, examining the disconnected jack*) Out, I see.

**CHARLIE** In a manner of speaking.

**GENE** Anyway, I was worried.

**CHARLIE** And you rushed right over, in the hopes of being the first to say, "I told you so." (*indicating wastebasket*) Congratulations. You made it.

**GENE** Roses. Jesus.

**CHARLIE** You want to look at the card?

**GENE** (*looking her in the eye*) "No regrets. No blame. No bitterness." Something along those lines?

**CHARLIE** (*after a pause*) Say, did I ever tell you the one about the dumb broad, the professional bastard and the professional bastard's know-it-all younger brother?

**GENE** Let me tell you one. Nick never promised you anything. So you've come out ahead. If you count the flowers as a bonus.

**CHARLIE** Don't you stick up for him.

**GENE** He's my brother, Charlie. He has his faults, and I'm sorry if he hurt you but he tried to play straight with you and you know it.

**CHARLIE** Am I supposed to thank you for pointing that out?

**GENE** No, but you could offer me a drink.

**CHARLIE** Not if you've come here to gloat.

**GENE** No.

**CHARLIE** In that case, have a drink. (*unscrewing the top from the last bottle of wine*) Care to smell the cap?

**GENE** Where did all these bottles come from?

**CHARLIE** The liquor store sends their empties over. I'm too young to drink, of course. But I like my garbage to look adult.

**GENE** (*taking a swig of wine*) My favourite. Melted cough drops.

**CHARLIE** If you don't like the house wine, don't blame me. I stole it from my neighbour. He's out of town and I'm feeding his cat. Of course, we can always try our luck with the neighbour on the other side. I'm watering her plants. (*shaking a key ring*) The keys to the kingdom, baby.

**GENE** How much of this did you drink tonight?

**CHARLIE** All of it.

**GENE** All of it? Holy shit. Charlie, are you all right?

**CHARLIE** Never better. Oh, the day's had its ups and downs, I don't deny it. But I'm feeling better now. I had a good cry, I guess, and a little nap, and now I'm even working on the act. (*switching on the tape, singing into the mike*) You can trust the products at the Esso sign — (*but as* GENE *regards her steadily, she switches off the tape*) Oh well, a little later, maybe. (*close to tears*) After a cigarette. You got one, by any chance?

**GENE** (*handing her a cigarette*) You're in no mood to work on the act now.

**CHARLIE** I know. But maybe that's no excuse.

**GENE** Charlie, that doesn't make much sense.

**CHARLIE** I don't know. I was thinking tonight, about this comic they brought up from L.A. one time to headline at The Canada Goose. There was this one night, the show hadn't gone very well at all. And he invited three or four of the comics — young guys and me — back to his hotel room. He said he wanted to smoke dope and forget about the way the act had gone. But you know what happened when we got back to the hotel room?

**GENE** What?

**CHARLIE** The headliner brought out the dope all right, but, while the rest of us smoked it and watched the gangsters on The Late Show, the comic just sat in a corner, all alone, and played the tapes of his act. The room was a mess — dried-up old pizza crusts and coffee cups and cigarette butts. But the comic just sat there in the mess, with a stop-watch, and a notepad, and played the tapes.

**GENE** So what did the rest of you do?

**CHARLIE** What could we do? He was the headliner from L.A. So after every line, somebody would say, "That's a funny bit, man. That's very funny." And gradually the headliner began to pay attention to the fact that we were there, and he started throwing out new lines he'd spun off from the stuff on the tape. And after every line, he'd stop and ask, "What about that? Could that be funny?" Some of it was funny and some of it wasn't, but we told him it was dynamite and he wrote it down. I think that he was afraid that if he stopped he'd die. You know, the way a shark has to keep moving or die? I think he was afraid that if he stopped he'd be consumed by the garbage in the hotel room, or the ambition of the young comics coming up behind him, or the brutality of The Late Show.

**GENE** But he was the one who messed up the room. He was the one who invited you in and turned on the TV.

**CHARLIE** That's right. (*pausing*) I wonder. Maybe he actually needed that awfulness around him for incentive. Maybe he needed some place like that, that he had to be funny in or die.

**GENE** Could be.

**CHARLIE** So, maybe this is no time for me to stop. Maybe I've got to keep going now, or die.

GENE *clicks on the tape recorder and speaks into the mike.*

**GENE** Charlie, you're not going to die. Not tonight, anyway. (*clicking it off*) There. Now you've got it on tape. Play it back whenever you need reassurance.

**CHARLIE** That's the worst part of being a comedian. Everybody just laughs at you. (*as* GENE *laughs*) See what I mean?

**GENE** You're priceless. You really are.

**CHARLIE** You're not so bad yourself. I've always liked you, Gene.

**GENE** Now, there's a case of revisionist history.

**CHARLIE** After that first morning, I mean. And you were right. To give me a word of warning.

**GENE** It could be worse. You could be in love with him.

**CHARLIE** Who says I'm not?

**GENE** I do. What do you say?

**CHARLIE** (*after a pause*) No. I toyed with the possibility, while we were in the restaurant today and I realized he was looking for a way to kiss me off. I came very close to being in love with him, out of pure spite. But I'm not. It's more of a fascination, I guess. How anybody with so many connections can be so unconnected to anything. Women fall for stuff like that.

**GENE** Yeah? I'll make a note of it.

**CHARLIE** No, don't. Don't you turn into one of those half-assed eighties people. There are enough of them already. I guess we used up our quota of commitment in the sixties. Now we always keep our options open, as my late husband would say.

**GENE** And what does he mean by that?

**CHARLIE** Someday, sonny, when you're older, you'll understand.

**GENE** Do you?

**CHARLIE** No.

**GENE** Then you're not one of those people either, are you?

**CHARLIE** Gene, why did you come here tonight?

**GENE** I never miss a chance to sing the Happy Motoring Song.

**CHARLIE** Is that all?

**GENE** I like you, Charlie. I always have.

**CHARLIE** Now, there's a case of revisionist history.

**GENE** Seriously, from the first minute I saw you, I said to myself, "Now, there's a woman I could quit law school for."

**CHARLIE** Bullshit. You quit law school to become the greatest novelist the world has ever known. You told me so yourself.

**GENE** Charlie, you've got to learn to take a compliment.

**CHARLIE** I want to know why you came here.

**GENE** You mean, did Nick send me? No.

**CHARLIE** You mean he's not in the habit of passing along his old girlfriends? Like hockey skates? I wouldn't put it past him.

**GENE** You ought to think a little better of me.

**CHARLIE** I'm sorry.

**GENE** So am I.

**CHARLIE** Are you?

**GENE** Sorry. (*kissing her*) Sorry. (*kissing her again*) Sorry.

*And again.* CHARLIE *pulls away.*

**GENE** Uh … that's not exactly how I planned my move.

**CHARLIE** This isn't quite how I saw today shaping up either.

**GENE** Charlie, this may come as a surprise to you, but you're not a pair of hockey skates.

**CHARLIE** Is that one of those compliments I'm supposed to learn how to take?

**GENE** If I'd wanted wisecracks, I'd have stayed at The Canada Goose.

**CHARLIE** And if I'd wanted to save my sanity, I'd have stayed away from the Bolton boys.

**GENE** I'm not one of the Bolton boys. I'm Gene. And what went wrong with you and Nick has nothing to do with me.

**CHARLIE** You mean, don't throw out the baby with the bathwater? (*suddenly laughing*) Oh God, I'm sorry … (*still laughing*) I just realized what I said.

**GENE** (*sharply*) Charlie, I said cut the cracks. I'm not a baby and I'm not the relief pitcher or any other goddamn thing you think. And if you had any kind of decent opinion of yourself, I wouldn't have to tell you that.

**CHARLIE** (*staring at him uncertainly*) Gene … Do you want to sleep with me?

**GENE** It's crossed my mind. From time to time. To time.

**CHARLIE** Why?

**GENE** What kind of question is that?

**CHARLIE** I mean, why am I not a pair of hockey skates?

**GENE** (*earnestly*) Listen to me. I don't make a habit of chasing around after the recently broken-hearted, knocking on the door —

**CHARLIE** You didn't knock —

**GENE** Knocking on the door and offering myself as the consolation prize. You attract me, all right? You always have. In spite of your neuroses and your bad taste in men and your habit of calling me sonny. And right now, I can't think of anything nicer than being in bed with you. I can't see how it can fail as a bright idea.

**CHARLIE** But?

**GENE** I didn't say but.

**CHARLIE** You were thinking but. I saw it, in one of those balloons, over your head.

**GENE** But I'm not like Nick and all the open-option people. Gene. The name is Gene. I want you to have that straight in the morning. And the morning after. And the morning after that. What do you say, Charlie?

CHARLIE *switches on the tape, picks up the mike.*

**CHARLIE** (*into the mike*) Gene. I have it straight. And I'll have it straight in the morning. (*clicking off the tape*) There. Now you've got it on tape. Play it back when you need reassurance. (*taking off her glasses*) Your turn. Fair is fair.

GENE *takes off his glasses, then picks up* CHARLIE'*s, looks through them.*

**GENE** You're as blind as I am.

**CHARLIE** This could be the beginning of a beautiful friendship.

CHARLIE *leans towards* GENE *and he kisses her on a blackout.*

## Act Two, Scene One

*A day or two later. Lights come up on* GENE *at his desk, speaking into his tape recorder.*

**GENE** *"Deathless Prose"* by Eugene Bolton. Chapter One. It came as a surprise to him to realize that this was what being in love felt like. He'd imagined the feeling many times, of course, and it had been different. Better circumstances, more exotic locations, a different kind of woman. For he wasn't so caught up in emotion that he couldn't admit that to himself. He'd simply never expected to fall, when he fell, for a woman like her. She was taller than what he'd had in mind, she smoked too much, and she was absolutely nothing like Jane Fonda. And she was older than he was. Most of all, she was older. And while it was nice to be around someone imbued with the kind of wisdom that only comes with age — like knowing all the lyrics to old Everly Brothers songs, and understanding more than he would ever know about how to fold a fitted sheet — while it was nice to have a shortcut to that kind of knowledge, it was also true that she'd had more time to accumulate bad memories. They'd talked about that, of course. They'd talked about it exhaustively until, sometimes, it seemed to him that was what new relationships mostly consisted of — performing autopsies on relationships from the past. (*breaking off*) Hey, that's not bad. I wonder if it's true? (*back to business*) Anyway, the more

**GENE** they talked, the more often he caught himself wishing that he'd inherited a prize somewhat more intact, emotionally speaking. Because almost from the first moment, a terrible suspicion had begun to form in him that, in the relationship game, you could actually be held accountable for debts run up long before you ever appeared on the scene. That he would be punished, somehow, for having turned up too late.

*Blackout.*

## Act Two, Scene Two

*A day or two later. Lights up on* CHARLIE's *apartment. An anonymous figure is under the covers of the bed. There is a knock on the door, a pause, another knock. Finally a credit card comes sliding through the lock, the door opens and* ALAN *enters, carrying his suitcase. He puts down the suitcase, approaches the bed.*

**ALAN** Charlie. Baby, wake up.

GENE *starts, sits up.*

**GENE** Who the hell are you?

**ALAN** (*startled*) I could ask you the same question.

**GENE** You don't know who you are? (*coming to*) Oh, right. I see.

**ALAN** Look — I'm sorry.

**GENE** It's okay. I know the feeling.

**ALAN** Where's Charlie? You do know who Charlie is?

**GENE** She was here … Holy shit. I have to be at work at twelve!

**ALAN** (*consulting his watch*) It's eleven-o-six.

**GENE** Oh, lots of time. (*lying back down in the bed, pulling the covers over himself*)

**ALAN** Look, is she okay?

**GENE** Charlie? (*smiling*) She's fantastic.

CHARLIE, *fully dressed except for her glasses, appears from the kitchen with two cups of coffee. She stops short when she sees* ALAN.

**CHARLIE** Alan! What are you doing here?

**ALAN** (*indicating* GENE *with chagrin*) Charlie, for Christ's sake …

**CHARLIE** Alan, this is Gene.

**GENE** Oh, you're Charlie's late husband. (*shaking hands*) Nice to meet you. Gene Bolton.

**ALAN** (*to* CHARLIE) Bolton?

**CHARLIE** Nick's brother. You remember Nick.

**ALAN** Better than you, evidently. Well, isn't this just jolly?

**GENE** We think so. (*indicating the coffee*) Is that mine?

CHARLIE *hands him a coffee, proffers the other to* ALAN.

**CHARLIE** Coffee, sweetheart? Or should I break out the Digitalis? (*as he takes the coffee, she peers at his suitcase*) Why, Alan, I didn't know you had a dog.

**ALAN** Put on your glasses, will you? It's my suitcase.

**CHARLIE** My God. I hope you boys have name tags sewn in your clothes. (*as no one laughs*) I wasn't expecting to see you.

**ALAN** Evidently.

**CHARLIE** Will you stop saying "evidently?" You sound like you've dropped in from Scotland Yard.

**ALAN** I dropped in from Stratford, Charlie. A mere three hours on a very slow train. Because I thought you needed me.

**CHARLIE** (*puzzled*) That's very sweet of you. But I'm just fine.

**ALAN** You didn't sound fine when you called me the other night.

**CHARLIE** The other night?

**ALAN** Christ, after that conversation, I rushed down here expecting to find you in a coma, not in flagrante delicto.

**CHARLIE** Sorry to disappoint you. Besides, nobody's in flagrante anything. Gene, put your clothes on.

**ALAN** I bet you don't remember a goddamn thing about that call, do you?

**CHARLIE** Sure I do. I — I guess it was about Nick?

**ALAN** You guess. Your heart was broken, I'd let you down too, and when I tried to call back —

**CHARLIE** Oh God. The jack. (*going to the phone, plugging it in*)

**ALAN** I've been calling on the hour, and wondering if I could get here before the ambulance.

**CHARLIE** Oh, sweetheart. I'm sorry.

**GENE** It took you three days to come a hundred miles? Were you really that concerned?

**CHARLIE** Gene …

**ALAN** Under the circumstances, it's a good thing I didn't run out to the highway and flag down a police car, isn't it?

**GENE** But there's no point carrying on as though you had, is there? I mean, I assume you were coming to Toronto anyway.

**ALAN** Well, there are people — (*angrily*) Look, what the hell business is this of yours?

**GENE** Charlie's business is my business now.

**ALAN** Well, good luck. Now that you've checked into the Hotel California, you'll need it.

**CHARLIE** Thanks for the glowing reference. I am sorry about the call. But I was drunk and —

**ALAN** (*joining in*) — and don't remember a thing about it. Charlie, when is this stuff going to stop?

**CHARLIE** I think it's stopped. This time I really think it has.

**ALAN** (*glancing at* GENE) I see. That's good, then. (*getting up*) Pardon the intrusion, as we say at Scotland Yard.

**CHARLIE** Where are you going?

**ALAN** Where do I usually go from here? To see if there are any other inns in Bethlehem. (*pausing, then defensively*) I mean, since I came all the way to town, I might as well stay for a day or two.

**CHARLIE** (*smiling*) You might as well. If you do have people to see, I'd feel a lot less guilty.

**ALAN** I can drop in on Grant Austin.

**CHARLIE** Good. Don't run away. I'll put on more coffee. (*exiting*)

**ALAN** Anyway, Grant will put me up, probably.

**GENE** If not, you could stay here. It's not like I'm moved in officially. I can go back home for a day or two.

**ALAN** No thanks.

**GENE** I don't mind. I mean, it's not like — (*stopping short, busying himself tying his shoes*)

**ALAN** It's not like what? It's not like having another man staying here?

**GENE** I didn't say that.

**ALAN** You don't have to. I'm a mind reader. So Charlie's told you all about me?

**GENE** The subject's come up. Look, Alan, I only meant everything's in the past with you and Charlie.

**ALAN** Everything's in the past? Did she say that?

**GENE** No, I'm a mind reader too. I see a couple separated for a year, I'm enjoying a gorgeous relationship with the lady, the guy's living with some other guy — I just had a wild hunch.

**ALAN** (*after a pause*) Coming out, you know, it's not like having a personality transplant. Some part of me is still her husband.

**GENE** (*gently*) That must be confusing.

**ALAN** It is. (*smiling ruefully*) As you point out, it takes me three days to show up after one of her calls, but I show up.

**GENE** Well … A wife in your past. Maybe it's comforting in a way?

**ALAN** Maybe it is. But maybe it's time to stop.

**GENE** Maybe it is.

**ALAN** Yeah. (*pausing*) I'm glad about you and her. I honestly am. It simplifies things a little.

**GENE** From the byzantine to the merely baroque?

**ALAN** (*smiling*) Something like that.

CHARLIE *returns with a coffee pot and her own cup.*

**CHARLIE** I knew there was more mileage in those grounds. Gene?

**GENE** Sounds irresistible, but I have to get to work. A salesclerk's life isn't his own.

**CHARLIE** You won't forget to call me on your break?

**GENE** Not likely. The one time I forgot, I got calls all afternoon in different accents. From women claiming to be customers I'd seduced and abandoned.

**CHARLIE** (*innocently*) No kidding?

**GENE** No kidding. You do a lousy Russian, by the way.

**CHARLIE** (*Russian*) Pah, ees stinking lie. (*in her own voice*) Smartass.

**GENE** Bitch. (*kissing her*) Alan — nice meeting you. (*exiting* )

**CHARLIE** (*pouring* ALAN *more coffee*) Well.

**ALAN** Well, what can I say? You hit the jackpot this time.

**CHARLIE** You really think so?

**ALAN** Come on, he loves you. Anybody can see that.

**CHARLIE** He's very young.

**ALAN** Obituaries in advance? It won't work with him.

**CHARLIE** You don't think it's a bit silly — working my way through Nick's family?

**ALAN** Babe, it has nothing to do with me. It's time we both admitted that. (*rising*)

**CHARLIE** There's a tone of finality there I don't like. (*quickly*) I poured you more coffee. You can't leave.

**ALAN** Someone's got to tell you: your coffee's not worth hanging around for. (*kissing her*) Be happy.

**CHARLIE** (*nervously*) There's that tone again.

**ALAN** Why are we so stubborn? The sun goes down, and we still won't call it a day. (*picking up his suitcase*)

**CHARLIE** Alan —

**ALAN** 'Bye, Charlie.

ALAN *exits, leaving* CHARLIE *a little startled on a blackout.*

## Act Two, Scene Three

*Four weeks later. Lights come up on* CHARLIE's *apartment, where she sits typing desultorily, and crossing words out repeatedly. The phone rings.*

**CHARLIE** Thank God for interruptions. (*picking up phone*) Hello? (*pausing, Italian accent*) Yeah, whatchoo want onna pizza? (*pausing*) Yeah. (*pausing*) Yeah. (*pausing*) No. No anchovies, we no got today. Gino, he still out inna boat. Ciao.

CHARLIE *hangs up.* GENE *has come in from the kitchen during the conversation. He has a dish towel tied around his waist, wipes his hands on it.*

**GENE** They want Tower of Pizza?

**CHARLIE** Who else? Since they opened, nobody ever calls for us. (*unplugging the phone*) This time, I'm leaving it off. Until one of us gets a new number. I wouldn't mind if people didn't get so ugly about the anchovies.

**GENE** Guy called earlier, wanted orange sections. On a pizza. It's enough to make you want to get out of the catering business all right.

**CHARLIE** Speaking of which, how's dinner coming?

**GENE** Later. I'm still working on the fridge. Haven't you ever heard of defrosting?

**CHARLIE** You live here too, you know.

**GENE** I've only been here a month. I won't say how long it's been since that fridge was touched but there's a hunk of frozen fish in there wrapped in newspaper. Headline says: "White Sox Throw World Series." (*as* CHARLIE *laughs*) Anyway, there's no rush on dinner. Nick isn't even coming till eight.

**CHARLIE** At this point, I'm ready to start without him. Any excuse to drop this. (*picking up a piece of her writing, reads*) "It's no use, Jerry. We can't get married as long as Alison's ghost stands between us. After all, if she hadn't killed herself because you left her for me, it would be her you'd be taking to the altar Wednesday morning."

**GENE** She.

**CHARLIE** What?

**GENE** It would be she you'd be taking to the altar Wednesday morning. There's your problem right there.

**CHARLIE** The problem is, Alison's suicide has nothing to do with Jerry. Alison was carrying Leonard Casey's child and, somehow, I've got to tip off Ruth and Jerry to that. Otherwise nobody goes to the altar Wednesday morning.

**GENE** Well, Wednesday is a stupid day for a wedding anyway.

**CHARLIE** It happens to be Jerry's day off. He works Saturdays. At The Bay.

**GENE** Yeah? How come the bastard didn't invite me to the wedding?

**CHARLIE** They're keeping it small. In deference to Alison. And there isn't going to be any wedding. Not unless I can get the truth out to somebody.

**GENE** Leonard Casey might have a word with Jerry.

**CHARLIE** He might — if they hadn't croaked him at the last story conference. On Thursday's show, Leonard's brakes will fail. On Friday, the actor goes into rehearsal in New York.

**GENE** It just goes to show. How fleeting is death.

**CHARLIE** Look, we can't all be novelists, sonny.

**GENE** They called again from The Canada Goose.

**CHARLIE** What do they want on their pizza?

**GENE** Mel called to find out if he could book you for a night next week.

**CHARLIE** What's the point? I haven't got any new stuff.

**GENE** There's old stuff, isn't there?

**CHARLIE** I have to feel that I want to be there, that's all. Otherwise, it might as well be soap opera.

**GENE** Well, wait until you feel like it, then.

**CHARLIE** Easy for you to say. How many chapters have you knocked out in the last few weeks?

**GENE** A couple.

**CHARLIE** Only a couple. On top of a full-time job. While I don't know what comes after, "Hi, everybody, and welcome to The Canada Goose."

**GENE** Charlie, what's the matter? I thought you were happy.

**CHARLIE** It's always hard to cope with the new and bizarre.

**GENE** Is that why you asked Nick to dinner? Out of nostalgia for the bad old days?

**CHARLIE** Do you think it's a bad idea?

**GENE** You, me and Nick? It smacks of such modernity, that's all. "Have Your Ex Over to Dinner to Meet Your Current." It would make a great story for Toronto Life.

**CHARLIE** Toronto Life is a contradiction in terms.

**GENE** Don't change the subject.

**CHARLIE** Why should there be hard feelings between you and Nick and me? Everybody's got what they want.

*There is a knock on the door.*

**GENE** Christ. Eight o'clock I told the asshole. It's five to. Some people have no consideration whatso — (*opening the door to admit* NICK) Nicky! Good to see you. Champagne! You finally off the penicillin?

NICK *presents the champagne to* CHARLIE *along with a kiss.*

**NICK** Hiya, Charlie. Bubbly to bubbly.

**CHARLIE** The usual bottle of Baby Bear, I see.

**NICK** If you don't like Dom Perignon, there are plenty who do.

**CHARLIE** It's just that every time you turn up, I feel I should have an unlaunched ship on hand.

**NICK** I bought it to launch the new picture. But now it looks like shooting's postponed. So I figured you two could use it.

**GENE** Second-hand champagne. How tacky. I'm sorry about the film, Nick.

**NICK** (*indicating* GENE's *dish towel*) I'm sorry I missed the drag show, little brother.

**GENE** I was cleaning the fridge.

**NICK** Well, no need to ask what brought you two together.

**GENE** The screwdrivers I made froze solid. It was time for a little defrosting.

**NICK** Okay, but you know what the fridge-cleaning syndrome leads to.

**CHARLIE** Nick, we didn't get you over here to reminisce. We're all familiar with the past and presumably none of us is too wild about it. (*taking the champagne*) I'll get you a screwdriver popsicle. (*exiting*)

**GENE** (*firmly*) I'm making the dinner. We might as well have that out in the open too. (*exiting*)

CHARLIE *returns momentarily with a frozen pitcher of screwdrivers and two glasses.*

**CHARLIE** One lump or two? (*prodding at the pitcher*)

**NICK** However it comes. I only see two glasses.

**CHARLIE** I'm not drinking these days, Nick. And you know something? I thought sobriety would be awful. It's not. It's hideous.

**NICK** Then you might as well have a drink.

**CHARLIE** Later.

**NICK** Later?

**CHARLIE** A week Thursday. That'll be a month. I promised myself a month on the wagon.

**NICK** But babe, you were always such a fun drunk.

**CHARLIE** Such a load of laughs that you dropped me.

**NICK** Aw now, don't be that way. I felt rotten that day in the restaurant.

**CHARLIE** Your pain showed. As I recall it, you said, "We're through, Charlie. I wonder if the artichokes are any good today?"

**NICK** Bullshit, I did not.

**CHARLIE** You're right. But I never let the truth spoil a good story yet.

**NICK** No brother of Gene's can be that bad. After all, I raised that kid practically single-handed. If he didn't learn decency from me, where did he learn it?

**CHARLIE** He probably had to pick it up in the streets.

*There is a knock on the door.*

**CHARLIE** Are they coming to take out pizzas here now?

CHARLIE *opens the door as* ALAN, *harried, steps in.*

**ALAN** So you are home. I've been calling and calling and —

**CHARLIE** Oh, right. We get all these wrong numbers, so I've been leaving it off.

**NICK** Hi, Alan.

**ALAN** Oh, hi, Nick. (*bewildered*) How are you?

**CHARLIE** (*plugging the phone in*) There. Now try your call again.

**ALAN** I don't know why you bother having a phone, Charlie.

**CHARLIE** Who are you? A field worker from the Telephone Appreciation Society?

**NICK** What this man needs is a drink. And a glass. (*exiting*)

**ALAN** I don't have time for — (*but* NICK *is gone*) Charlie, do you still have that metal box we kept all the valuable papers in?

**CHARLIE** I've got the box, but you took all your papers out, remember? When we split up.

**ALAN** Can you look? I think I must have left my passport. I've got to have it.

**CHARLIE** Why? Where are you going?

**ALAN** I won't be going anywhere if you don't look in the goddamn box! (*as* CHARLIE *doesn't budge.*) Spain.

**CHARLIE** Spain? What with? I mean, I hear it's cheap there, but it can't be free. Or who with? Maybe that's more to the point?

**ALAN** Grant Austin.

**CHARLIE** You're kidding.

**ALAN** Now that I've answered the skill-testing question, can I have my passport?

**CHARLIE** You and Grant Austin. So good old Jackie's out in the cold?

**ALAN** Charlie, please! Just find my passport, and I'll tell you anything you want to know.

**CHARLIE** (*bitterly*) It never stops with you, does it?

**ALAN** It has now. This time it's stopped.

CHARLIE *stares at him for a moment, then exits swiftly.* ALAN *lights a cigarette.* NICK *comes back with a glass, pours* ALAN *a screwdriver from the slightly-melted batch.*

**NICK** That kid. I never saw him so much as heat up a can of soup, and now he's out there up to his eyebrows in souffle. Souffle, for Christ's sake. Here you go. (*handing* ALAN *a screwdriver*)

**ALAN** Thanks. (*gulping it, checking his watch*)

**NICK** You in a hurry to get somewhere?

**ALAN** Yeah. Spain.

**NICK** Spain? Lot of that going around. Remember Grant Austin? The fucker's walked off the picture to go to Spain.

**ALAN** Is that a fact?

**NICK** Jesus, I should have known. The guy may be a cinematic genus, but he goes down the road of life using *True Confessions* as a driving manual. I call him up and ask him what the hell he thinks he's doing to me, and you know what he tells me? He's in love.

**ALAN** (*coldly*) It happens.

*At this moment* CHARLIE *comes back to the doorway with the passport, unnoticed for the moment.*

**NICK** Yeah, Grant's in love with some cute little fruit. And after some little faggot wedding ceremony they're honeymooning in Spain.

**CHARLIE** A gay wedding? (*to* ALAN, *with deep distaste*) A wedding?

**ALAN** (*reaching for the passport*) You found it. Great.

**CHARLIE** (*slamming it into his hand*) I found it all right.

**NICK** Yeah, how about that, Charlie? There's material there for you. Can you see the wedding cake? Two little guys in tuxes under a flowered arch!

**ALAN** Why don't you just fuck off?

**CHARLIE** Why should he? It's pretty funny at that, Alan. I wish I'd been there to see you go down the aisle. Why wasn't I invited to the wedding? But of course, how do you seat the groom's wife? Or is it

**CHARLIE** the bride's wife? I guess Amy Vanderbilt doesn't cover that one.

**NICK** Oh Christ. Charlie, I didn't know. Alan ...

*At this moment* GENE *enters from the kitchen*

**GENE** My souffle just fell. Who did it?

**NICK** (*quietly*) I did it. I put my foot in it.

**CHARLIE** My God, if you wanted a divorce, you could have said so. Or would you rather conduct secret ceremonies behind my back? Just to make sure I'm really out of the picture?

**ALAN** What do you care what I do now? Why should it matter to you? You're living with him, for God's sake — (*indicating* GENE) He drops in for drinks — (*indicating* NICK) You think you can hold onto everybody?

**CHARLIE** You do it, don't you? That's always been your stock in trade.

**ALAN** Not any more! It's a day, Charlie. Why can't we just call it that?

**CHARLIE** Because it isn't! You need me, Alan. If only to trot out for state occasions.

**ALAN** Not any more. If anybody wants to think of me as a fruit, or a faggot or a fucking queer, they can go ahead. I've made my peace with it. And I'm not taking the blame any more for the tragedy of poor little Charlie, victim of the Evil Homosexual Conspiracy. There were a hundred things wrong with our marriage and if I'd stayed as straight as Charles Bronson, we'd have fallen apart anyway.

**CHARLIE** That's not true.

**ALAN** It's true and you know it. But now you've got someone who loves you and so do I. So let's let go. Before we guilt each other to death. Let me go, Charlie.

ALAN *touches her arm briefly, pockets the passport and leaves.* GENE *and* NICK *stare warily at* CHARLIE *as if she were a bomb about to explode.*

**GENE** (*at last*) Charlie? …

**CHARLIE** He's going all the way to Spain. And he didn't even say goodbye.

**GENE** He said goodbye. You know it.

**NICK** Christ, Charlie, I didn't know. You never told me anything about it.

**CHARLIE** I know. Look, why don't you guys go ahead with dinner? I'd like to take a walk.

**GENE** Now? Come on, why don't you —

**CHARLIE** (*snatching up her purse*) I need this walk, Gene. I really do.

CHARLIE *hurries out, slamming the door.*

**GENE** Oh, Christ. (*to* NICK) What the hell did you do?

**NICK** I mentioned Austin walked off the picture to marry some little fruit. How did I know it was Alan? Come on, kid. Relax. A week from Thursday has probably come a little early, that's all.

**GENE** She was through getting drunk over him. That was all behind her.

**NICK** Then you don't have to worry about her, right?

**GENE** You don't know a goddamn thing about it.

**NICK** You will pardon me but I do have some experience of the lady. And a few others just like her.

**GENE** She's not just "some lady" — some back number in your little black book. She's Charlie, Nick, and you've got no idea. I mean, you didn't even know Alan was gay.

**NICK** Maybe not. But I know one thing, Geno, and you'd better deal with it — she just jumped at the chance to go to pieces tonight. And if she's looking for ways to be unhappy, there's nothing you can do about it.

**GENE** Stop right there, Nick, because I'm not going to take it. Some underdone theory on another woman you scratched at the gate. I live with her, for Christ's sake. I've taken responsibility. And on that subject, I'm the big brother.

**NICK** Listen, you little wise-ass. I'll take a lot from you but not a lecture. Talk to me about responsibility! I put clothes on your back and a roof over you —

**GENE** And you felt virtuous as hell because I needed you! But not anymore. Now I've got someone who needs me. And a life of my own. Do you get that, Nick?

**NICK** Sure, sure. You're running your own show now — and making a real class job of it. Sitting at the door like a spaniel and whining because she's left you all alone. (*moving to the door*) No, you don't

**NICK** need me. Not much. Because all I ever gave you was cash and connections and everything you're too goddamned good for, right? But when I try to give you anything else — like some advice — you tell me to fuck right off. Okay, kid, you've got it. I'm gone.

**GENE** Nick! I — don't want you to go.

**NICK** Why? Because you're afraid to be here all alone?

**GENE** No. I — (*slowly*) I think maybe — I need some — advice.

**NICK** Could be. Could be I've considered a few angles you haven't. About having a life of your own.

**GENE** She's better off with me, Nick. Better off than she's been in her whole life. And she knows it.

**NICK** I don't deny it for a second. Anybody who can't be happy with you ought to have her head read.

**GENE** (*laughing weakly*) Yeah. That's what I think, too.

**NICK** Okay, but I got to thinking the other day. I was down at The Canada Goose, with some people who want to shoot a film. I asked after Charlie, and what do you know? Seems she hasn't shown up there in almost a month.

**GENE** I know. She hasn't felt like working lately.

**NICK** Why? Because she's up to her armpits in domestic bliss? Sure, I'll buy that. But it's funny how she only feels like performing when she's got a beef. Inconvenient, too.

**GENE** What do you mean?

**NICK** Well, she's got nothing to complain about now. With you on the premises — tossing up souffles and, I trust, keeping her happy in the sack the way only you undergraduates can. I mean, it's the ideal arrangement all down the line. But what can someone like Charlie do with that?

**GENE** She can enjoy it, can't she? She's earned it.

**NICK** Right. Now she's better off. But does she want to be better off? Does she even know how to be? You're a good kid, Geno, and it's too early in the game to get tied to a losing situation. She wants to be a loser, she can be a loser without you.

**GENE** Either it clicks with a woman or it doesn't, is that it? No point in trying to talk about it?

**NICK** Oh hell, talk if you want to. But if you're bright, you'll make *her* do the talking. She's the one with the problem. And if you don't like what you're hearing, hit the road.

**GENE** Just like that.

**NICK** Just like that. There's only one way to go if you're going — fast. (*gently*) Hey, don't look like a house just fell on you. Nothing's happened yet. Relax, and drink your screwdriver before it melts.

NICK *raises his glass to* GENE *on a blackout.*

## Act Two, Scene Four

*The next morning. Lights up on* CHARLIE's *apartment where* GENE *is listlessly tidying up from the night before. The door unlocks, and* CHARLIE, *tired and dishevelled, enters. She starts a little when she sees GENE.*

**GENE** That was some walk.

**CHARLIE** It was a little longer than I'd planned.

**GENE** Fourteen hours. What did you do, jog out to the airport and back?

**CHARLIE** I'm sorry if you were worried. You didn't skip work on account of me?

**GENE** It's my day off. Wednesday. Remember? (*pausing*) Are you okay?

**CHARLIE** I ... didn't expect to find you here, that's all. I planned to just crawl in and sleep.

**GENE** You can do that. You can do whatever you want.

**CHARLIE** You're not mad at me for staying out? I'd be mad. I'd be mad as hell.

**GENE** (*after a pause*) The souffle didn't fall after all. It just buckled at the knees a little. Nick was impressed, in spite of himself.

**CHARLIE** What?

**GENE** Last night's dinner. You missed it.

**CHARLIE** Oh, right ...

**GENE** I tried to save you some. Except once the fridge got the knack of defrosting, it went hog wild. The butter started melting. A few eggs hatched.

**CHARLIE** (*absently*) That's too bad.

**GENE** Yeah, I think the fridge is fucked. But Nick said —

**CHARLIE** Gene, don't you want to know where I went?

**GENE** Not unless you want to discuss it. Anyway, Nick said if we were in the market for a new fridge, he knows some guy —

**CHARLIE** I went to a bar and I started drinking. That's the last thing I remember until this morning —

**GENE** So you fell off the wagon.

**CHARLIE** (*relentlessly*) Until this morning when some guy I'd never seen before shook me awake and told me he'd drive me to the subway because he had to be at work by nine.

**GENE** Okay, so now you've told me.

**CHARLIE** For Christ's sake, is that all you've got to say?

**GENE** What else do you want me to say?

**CHARLIE** What the hell kind of question is that? What do you feel like saying? I mean, you are entitled to get mad, you know. At the very least you're entitled to raise your voice!

| | |
|---|---|
| **GENE** | Why? Because you've got this little trick switch in your mind that allows you to check out whenever you feel like behaving like an asshole? Charlie, it's not worth getting mad about. It's stupid and it's sad, but beyond that it doesn't mean a thing. |
| **CHARLIE** | I don't know … |
| **GENE** | Yes you do, and if you want to tell me, let's get it over with. |
| **CHARLIE** | Gene, I wouldn't hurt you, not for the world … |
| **GENE** | I know that line. It's what you say just before you hurt someone. (*lightly*) So what's the story? You fell in love with this guy on the way to the subway station? |
| **CHARLIE** | No. It was when I saw Alan, Gene. I realized it's not over for me. |
| **GENE** | Well, it's over for him. And I love you. Why the hell do you want to louse it up? |
| **CHARLIE** | I don't want to louse it up … |
| **GENE** | But? But what? Come on, I can see it. In a balloon right over your head. |
| **CHARLIE** | Sorry, this just isn't working. |
| **GENE** | It's working for me. Sorry to be so uncooperative, but there it is. |
| **CHARLIE** | (*exasperated*) Look, you're seven years younger than I am, and sooner or later you're going to want to play with girls your own age. Then you'll walk out on me and — |

**GENE** Oh no you don't. You're the one walking, and don't try to pull that switch. I've told you I love you, and you've got no reason to think any different. So if you want to walk, fucking do it. But at least admit it's your own idea.

**CHARLIE** (*exploding*) How the hell can you want this? I'm screwed up and I drink too much and you're way too good for me.

**GENE** That's not the problem. You want to know what the problem is? The fact that I love you. You just can't deal with that. Because any club that would have you as a member just isn't good enough to join.

**CHARLIE** You don't know what you're talking about.

**GENE** Don't I? You think you want Alan. It's only because he doesn't want you. That's his entire attraction. All somebody has to do is dump you and you'll follow them anywhere.

**CHARLIE** It has nothing to do with what I want.

**GENE** It has everything to do with it because this time you're calling the shots. It's not as easy as being the victim, is it? And I have no intention of making it easy for you. Come on — go or stay? What do you want me to do? It's not enough to get loaded and pick up some guy in a bar and hope that'll turn me off. (*snatching up her tape recorder, switching it on, putting the mike in front of her*) You're going to have to tell me. Once and for all.

**CHARLIE** (*at last*) Gene, you'll be better off without me.

**GENE** (*snapping off the tape*) I asked for an answer, not bullshit! (*more calmly*) But I guess it's an answer

**GENE** all the same. (*reaching under the bed for his suitcase*)

**CHARLIE** I love you. I don't care if you believe it.

**GENE** You know what I believe? That this moment is the closest you've come to it since I first met you. And by the time I go through that door, you'll be there. Now tell me that isn't true.

**CHARLIE** I — (*covering her face with her hands*) I never wanted to hurt you, Gene. You're the best man I've ever met.

**GENE** I know. I only hope someday you'll find it in your heart to forgive me for it. (*as she touches his arm*) Let go of me. I need two arms to pack. In that respect I'm no better than any of the others.

*His perfunctory packing done,* GENE *closes the case and moves to the door.*

**CHARLIE** Gene …

**GENE** Do me one favour. Don't send roses okay?

GENE *leaves. Lights hold on* CHARLIE *for a moment, then blackout.*

## Act Two, Scene Five

*Some weeks later. Lights up on The Canada Goose where* CHARLIE *is onstage in her customary gear plus a feather boa, with the mike in her hand.*

**CHARLIE** Hey ladies, there's a big vogue now in younger men. You noticed that? I don't know about you, but I don't want to go out to dinner with someone who has to ask the waiter to bring him the Child's Menu. Okay, okay, so the kid CAN come ten times in a single night. So what? It's always over so quickly, right? It's like getting ten episodes of "*Leave It to Beaver*" — right in a row.

It beats the old guys, though. A session with your average older man is like a screening of *"The Sorrow and the Pity"*. Only longer and sadder. You nod off two or three times, and wake up, and he's STILL at it. "I almost came that time," he says. Eventually, you start trying to outfox him, right? "You came," you tell him. "You definitely came. It's just been so long you've forgotten what it's like. But that was it. Trust me. Now, can we get some sleep?"

But the real bitch about younger men is how goddamn earnest they are. One roll in the hay, and they're ready to move in—provided you're willing to help them with their algebra. And when you say, "Hey, wait a minute, sonny — " (*faltering on the name, breaking off for a moment, and then, almost to herself*) Sonny. (*long, baffled pause, then plunging on, almost desperately*) No, no, I prefer to stick to single guys my own age. Hey, has

**CHARLIE** anybody SEEN any single straight guys lately? You know they're an endangered species. (*gradually regaining composure*) In fact, I heard recently a woman was picketed on Bloor Street by the Greenpeace people for wearing a coat made of the pelts of single straight men.

But I actually met a single guy once. First thing he said to me was, "Babe — " He called all women Babe. I guess it eliminated the problem of learning names he'd only have to forget. "Babe," he said, "I'm not into involvement." And you know something? He wasn't. In fact, if you called him up when he was out, there was this message on his answering machine. "Hi, I'm not home right now. And I'm not into involvement." But I did manage to go out with him — once. And he said to me, "Babe, you chicks are all the same. You're takers." Some taker. We'd been out to dinner, where we split the tab. We split a taxi to the movie where I paid my own way, plus sprang for his popcorn. Now we're back at my place, doing it in my bed, drinking my Scotch and smoking my cigarettes — and I'm a taker? What do I have to do to be a giver? Donate my kidneys?

*Blackout on* CHARLIE. *Lights up on* GENE *at his desk speaking into his tape recorder*

**GENE** (*into the mike*) In fiction when people split up, they never see each other again. Their farewells are conveniently followed by a blank page or a closing credit roll. In real life, it works a little differently. For a while he avoided anything or any place that reminded him of her because fiction had taught him that was the right thing to do. But in the end, real life won out and he went down to the club where she performed and watched her unobtrusively from the back. And while he

**GENE** considered the things that she said to be specious and exaggerated, he did have to concede that she seemed happier up there, telling stories that featured her as the perpetual underdog, perpetually disappointed.

And as he watched her it occurred to him for the first time that perhaps he'd got what he wanted too. That losing not only makes for better prose but is, in the long run, safer than winning. Safe being a relative term, of course. There were, for instance, people who considered it unsafe to set foot in an airplane. And yet he knew for an absolute certainty that it was a hell of a lot more dangerous down on the ground.

*Blackout.*

*The End.*